I Still Believe in Miracles

I Still Believe in Miracles

Poems to Find Meaning in Difficult Times

LUCAS JONES

EBURY PRESS

EBURY PRESS

UK | USA | Canada | Ireland | Australia
India | New Zealand | South Africa

Ebury Press is part of the Penguin Random House group of companies
whose addresses can be found at global.penguinrandomhouse.com

Penguin Random House UK
One Embassy Gardens, 8 Viaduct Gardens, London SW11 7BW

penguin.co.uk

First published by Ebury Press in 2026

9

Copyright © Lucas Jones 2026
The moral right of the author has been asserted.

Penguin Random House values and supports copyright. Copyright fuels creativity, encourages diverse voices, promotes freedom of expression and supports a vibrant culture. Thank you for purchasing an authorised edition of this book and for respecting intellectual property laws by not reproducing, scanning or distributing any part of it by any means without permission. You are supporting authors and enabling Penguin Random House to continue to publish books for everyone. No part of this book may be used or reproduced in any manner for the purpose of training artificial intelligence technologies or systems. In accordance with Article 4(3) of the DSM Directive 2019/790, Penguin Random House expressly reserves this work from the text and data mining exception.

Typeset in 10.4/13.5pt Fleischman BT Pro by Six Red Marbles UK, Thetford, Norfolk

Printed and bound in Great Britain by Clays Ltd, Elcograf S.p.A.

The authorised representative in the EEA is Penguin Random House Ireland,
Morrison Chambers, 32 Nassau Street, Dublin D02 YH68

A CIP catalogue record for this book is available from the British Library

ISBN 9781529971491

Penguin Random House is committed to a sustainable future
for our business, our readers and our planet. This book is made
from Forest Stewardship Council® certified paper.

For my parents.
In infinite love.
For still and always believing.

Contents

Introduction — 1
Introduction: Director's cut — 3

I met God at the supermarket — 7
Pastel pink — 10
Note to Editor: I'll title this later — 11
This is how I speak — 13
Like the flower — 14
I'm doing this thing where I'm pretending to be nice to women — 15
I had a missed call from Grief — 17
Oh, I'm sorry for that thing that ruined your life — 18
In the elevator to heaven — 20
If nothing else — 21
What men get wrong about women — 22
I never thought about it but statistically someone bought my book and died — 23
There will be times when the world is too much — 24
I don't believe in presidents — 26
You're not in love, you're in pain — 28
If I could just get five minutes of not thinking about myself — 29
If he loved you, he would — 30
I'd never be a Nazi — 32
Today — 35
Has anyone checked on the boys? — 36
Maybe you didn't give up on your dreams — 38
Good people — 40
I had a message saying 'You saved my life' — 41
An unexpected consequence of healing — 42
Nothing hurts more than the joy of a woman — 43
Made it, made what — 44
One last bomb for freedom — 45
He asked me to write this before his girl dies — 46

My therapist said if you have depression and — 47
I had a comment the other day — 48
You do not have to say the right thing — 51
This country is an abusive parent — 53
Drop the slave name — 54
I still believe in love — 55
Billionaire internet boys' club — 56
The beautiful thing about dying is this — 57
Know this — 58
Don't tell the children — 59
The relationship's dead, where do we hide the body? — 60
The deradicalisation of a 21st-century man — 62
I saw God on the train — 65
Your boy's last compliment — 67
The man who died at his desk job — 68
You can't be a victim forever — 69
Me / ADHD — 70
It's the house with the balloons out front — 71
Doing okay checklist — 73
Love is a house that you build by the beach — 74
Activist [in bio] — 75
An artist is a hunter — 76
End Paragraph — 77
I'll always be raining — 78
Me if I die before my girl — 79
Have you heard the story of the Wolf and the Beach? — 80
No matter what you buy, you're only ever renting — 83
For anyone thinking 'I'll never love again' — 84
The King of Therapy — 86
Someone said I never criticise women — 88
Dating in the city — 92
Angel mum — 93
[A Hug After That Sad Poem] — 95
I might not get there with you — 96
Voting Day — 97
Who told you that love was easy? — 99
Why Me? — 101
I don't go on walks to cheer myself up — 103

In — 104
If you age seven could see you now — 105
How to kill a CEO — 106
You wouldn't understand — 108
Recovery — 110
Hunger — 111
No such thing as the one that got away — 116
They look down at us from up there — 117
The plot of *Dune* — 119
(all the mixed-race boys) Audition — 120
The world got smaller — 121
miracles — 122
Act III — 123
I found God at the funeral — 124

Acknowledgements — 127

Introduction

Firstly, thank you.

It's the most impossibly profound honour to know that, if you're reading this, you're holding this book in your hands. You could be spending your time and money anywhere else in the world, but you're choosing to spend it here. And, if you are here, maybe you kinda feel how I feel. Searching for meaning in these strange, lost days. Trying to find a way to access the love that's frozen under the ice of cynicism and post-modernism. Trying to find the words for that feeling.

I feel like I've spent my whole life so far trying to find a word for that feeling. As if there's a big red curtain drawn across the stage of reality, and only in the most precious, fleeting moments, do we get to see what's concealed behind it. Like falling in love. Surviving the death of a loved one. Seeing a friend's baby for the first time. Crying at the gig. Crying at the wedding. Crying.

I think, anytime we find ourselves scrolling through the chaos of the internet, we are attempting to find the words to understand it. Searching desperately for the next clip, post, news article that defines and colours our conscious experience. Some great discovery that awakens a dormant soul within us. For all of its flaws, there's something beautiful at the foundation of that. The physical paper pages you're holding are the manifestation of that. I'm a poet from the internet (on some days). All of this has come about because someone scrolled and liked a post. Someone shared it to their story. Someone saved it when their friend died. Someone clicked follow. And millions of identical moments later somehow it generated enough real-world meaning that you can now buy this physical book and put it on your physical bed, take a digital photo of it and post it online.

And I think, with zero cynicism, that this is a miracle.

It's a miracle that, despite having all of the world at your fingertips,

with every drug, every porn website, every cruel comment section, every endless, frivolous, fruitless darkness you could be involved in right now, you are choosing to be here: in the quiet introspection of a poetry book, trying to find the words.
So, thank you.

– Lucas

Introduction: Director's cut

Okay, now that's done, hello, fucking wow. All across the internet there were boys and girls all fast asleep and I used to dream of New York, and I actually did once cry on the subway – and nobody could tell. And I had a little cash. Some car commercial on the television that paid me more than anything I'd ever had or anyone I'd ever known.

(And I watched Penélope Cruz throw her arms up in the air and say, 'I'll see you in another life when we are both cats,' at probably . . . oh I don't know, age seven. And that was that – source code. That's in my blood forever. Now I understood love.)

And I was 90 per cent cut from the advert but my chin still made it in and on some beautiful insanity, some reason I can't claim, I still got paid what, at the time, may as well have been a million Queen's pounds.

So, I took my million and went to Brooklyn, then Manhattan, then the Gramercy Tavern and then I got a tattoo of that Bob Dylan album where he's kissing on that girl on the back of my leg. Went to Sofia Serrano's apartment location and saw it was for sale. Dreamed and dreamed and dreamt.

And the scene – I mean the moment – when I cried on the subway was mainly just from loneliness and I went to Mast bookshop and didn't buy anything. And I'm burning through my million. A million ain't gonna get you a hotdog round here boy, so afterwards I went to the fashion museum 'cos it was free or cheap, can't remember. And I wrote a poem there and I kept it in my pocket. I kept it where I keep all my past and my memories and all of my career, safely tucked up in my pocket.

And Fred Astaire's shoe collection was on display. And I had another panic attack – I kept having panic attacks around this time, too. And God, isn't it scary being alive and noticing? Choosing to love despite it all.

And when I got back to London, everything was rippling. I still lived in the countryside but somehow it was different. And I did this play – and you know sometimes it's fun to be sad, like tortured-poet-sad, knocking about Mayfair with a cake in a coat from your dad thinking, 'This is how Leonard Cohen felt. This is what "Morning Theft" by Jeff Buckley is about. This is what twenty-first-century diet pain feels like.'

Then I had a text from my landlord, like every other 20-something in the most expensive city in the world. Tryna cut a deal to keep a little life for myself, like, come on big man, let me buy food at least. Leave me not to the mice in the walls. I offered £725 – no dice, no deal. Settled on £850 per calendar month for a bedroom with a kitchen in it. Just expensive enough to die slowly enough to almost live.

And it really was a time I can't forget. Would never like to visit. Made a list of stuff I'm good at and didn't know how to fill it. Thought I'd better write myself away from here. Prayed with all my spirit.

And all my manic shit aside, all my meta-aphorisms put to sleep, that's the pain we're dealing with isn't it, really? If you sit at the end of your bed and really, really think on it, you know there is a hope-shaped hole in society. God's coffin hidden somewhere beneath the ocean. Beneath the fibre-optic cables carrying a 15-year-old's comment saying, 'Shut the fuck up' on a video of a man singing a little song he wrote with 409 views and 3 comments. And one of them says, 'Shut the fuck up'. And one of them says, 'Good job'. And one of them is a little thumbs up.

And you can call me a Pollyanna, but the thing that we must never let die is the wonder of it all. A child in August watching Penélope Cruz throw her arms in the air was enough to see it crystal clear. When we've finally cracked the code, split the atom, licked the algorithm, buried God, resurrected, filmed and killed him all over again; once we've finally broken it down to binary, praised and applauded every single man in a white lab coat, ripped up the coffin and finally, truly seen it; when we know now for certain without the darkest shadow's doubt, know now for certain the universe is empty; when all the world's news report:

'Heartbreaking News: it's just us, all alone.'
Then I hope you will read this listening to orchestral music slowly rising, the sun peeking over the mountain and the hairs on your arms reaching, reaching, remembering who you are.

On that sad death day, I'll stand with you at the edge of the end, with nothing but our phones. Hand in hand, at the depths of cynicism. Bleeding, broken, all out of tears.

And I'll cry with you ablaze:
I still believe in miracles.

I met God at the supermarket

He said 'You alright?'
I said 'Yeah, you?'
He goes 'What's on your mind?'
'Just getting some food'

But I think he could tell
'Cos I looked kinda sad
He said 'Go on then, ask'
I said 'Why are things bad?

Like, why is it hard?
Like, sometimes it's shit
Sometimes it's like
Oh my God is this it?'

He goes 'I can tell you that now
But you won't like the answer'
I said 'Don't give me riddles man
I'm not calling you "master"'

He said 'Fair enough,
I'll give it ya straight
You know in a film
Or a story or play

The bit when you think
It's all fucked, there's no way
The lead can survive then suddenly, yay
Something good happens
And then they're okay

And they learnt something true
And new on the way
Well, it's basically that
You'd be bored without this
You wouldn't know what the good bit is

Like what, just a film about
Someone who's fine
And then nothing happens
And wow, it's alright?'

He said 'Trust me, I've tried it
Before you were born
Where no one was rich
And no one was poor
And no one was cold
Just happy and warm

And it was so shit
They all went to war
Just to find reasons
To feel something more

So now it's like this
You hit then you miss
Then hit and then win
You know, that kinda thing'

And he could tell by my face
I was still kinda pissed
He said 'I tried to tell you
You wouldn't like the gift'

I said 'When does it end?'
He said 'Oh, in five minutes'
I said 'Wait, wait, what?
I've got so much to give

Just give me more time
I'm sorry, forgive !
My dreams are undreamt
Lost words on my lips

I missed all the sunsets
And clichés and shit
And loving my love
And time with my kids'

And then he goes
'Ahh, did someone find reason?
Look forward to something?
Have faith that there's meaning?'

I went 'Oh noooo
You got me, you prick'
He said 'Here's your time back
Now fuck off and live'

Pastel pink

Hair dye running down her cheeks
Like that Kate Moss photo in the blue towel
That little north-east London scene of girls
Sleeping in a single bed
Like that Chad Moore photo
When Amelia got pregnant for a bit
And Francis got sober / left that August

When Jamie split her lip, blood dripping (Diet Coke)
Like that James King photo, tights ripping on a rose
And crying in the cab, Alma nude on Danny's phone

Jamie on her birthday, two candles in a scone
At A&E then karaoke – 'You're the only love I've ever known'
Well some of them are married now with baby girls at home
And all that time together – we spent every day alone

Note to Editor: I'll title this later

Thank you, Penguin
I'm gonna put this one in the book
And I'll come back and title it
When I've worked it out

When I've got it and God has given it to me
When I've been let in and my children are
Happy and healthy
Inside the Anglo-American Dream

After fashion week and my per diems
Have been repaid and I am remade
In the image of a 1950s man
With every golden ornament

When I have sat at the church steps
Crying at the death I'm dying
Frightened, enlightened
Butchered and bastardised

When, and only when
The cash has been deposited
Spent, enjoyed, holiday'd, dreamt
And re-dreamt, borrowed, lent
And I start to resent

The man who wanted all of this
And had it and smashed it
On his marble floor by accident
Or in purpose, impassive

When I am wined, dined
Parking fined, have drawn the line
Of being really seriously finally dead

When the beauty and horror
Has gone to my head
And no one is left
No lover or friend

At the gates of Heaven
If I stand by what I said
Arrested by Angels
Silent in bed

That is the moment
Then and only then
Not one second sooner

Be it mountain or Hell
Or at a pub up in Soham
I will come back
And title this poem

This is how I speak

And how I speak is where I'm from
And where I've been is who I am
And who I am has stuff to say
And all of these things are inextractable
From each other

I talk like everyone I met on the way
And it's easier to rhyme when you mumble shit
Can make a metaphor thunderous
See what I mean, it takes elegance
I think *how* you say it's more relevant

The words are just really the sediment
To say it and mean it, that's medicine
So no, you can't have the sentiment
If your diction dictates the eloquence

Like the flower

You're lying here asleep in bed
I'm sitting on the floor
And everything I've loved in life
I love you so much more

**I'm doing this thing
where I'm pretending to be nice to women**

Like if she's going through something
I'll nod and I'll listen
And won't interrupt or tell her she's wrong

Sort of pretending to care and sometimes it's long
'Cos women will say stuff like 'Fuck patriarchy'
And I'll say 'Hey, do you feel safe at this party?
Is there anyone here making you feel uncomfortable?'

And usually there is
Then I'm right there to comfort you
As soon as her nurturing nature kicks in
She'll say 'You're so kind, you're not like other men'

And secretly, really, she has no idea
That I'm just pretending – I order two beers
Say 'Shall we fuck off? It's too loud in here'
(Implies that I'm sensitive) I whisper in her ear

And I keep up this act until she's at my place
'And I just want to say, there's no pressure to stay'
And then in the morning, I'll pretend to be sweet
And make her some breakfast if she wants to eat
And never once ever comment on her weight

Or make her feel scared – I'll pretend that she's safe
And pretend to be thoughtful and kind on our dates
And organise stuff, learn her likes and her hates
And traumas and triggers and meet her mum and her mates

Then I'll pretend she's the love of my life
Say 'Will you do me the honour of being my wife?'
And all of the bits that make women happy
Video it, post it – all that, exactly

And next I'll pretend that I want a family
A beautiful cloud of a house, be manly
Build stuff like . . . maybe a shed
Pretend to consider her needs with sex

Pretend to cry when our daughter exists
And look at her face through crocodile tears

Until basically I've got this pretend perfect home
Where my wife feels safe and she's never alone
And she's got no idea that I'm literally pretending
To raise my girl like an angel, defended

And it took 50-odd years
When she was dying and done
I sat by her bed, pretending we're one
Combing her hair, holding her thumb

And I won't care that her life is ending
'Cos things can't hurt you when you're just pretending
A fake lump in my throat, say 'I've got a confession
All of this time I've just been pretending'

And she goes 'Oh right? Love, are you tired?
You know I've lived such a beautiful life
All of this time, your love was so kind
In this infinite beauty of being your wife'
And I say 'Yeah, yeah, yeah. Okay, yeah right,
I love you' I say, while pretending to cry

And sometimes the air won't stay in my lungs
When our grandkids ask 'Where's Nana gone?'
And I just pretend that I feel I've been shot
Say 'She's just pretending she's dead
But she's not'

I had a missed call from Grief

I did see it ring
But didn't wanna pick up
I did see a bridge
Kinda did wanna jump

But instead I called back
'Cos love hates being missed
I said 'Yeah hello
Yeah I'm dealing with it'

'Cos grief always calls
Just when you forget
It stops when the love stops
Guess I'm not done yet

So I keep my phone on
And my messages checked
And I realise your life
Was the message you left

Oh, I'm sorry for that thing that ruined your life

You're right it's not fair, you were being so nice
And recycling stuff, watching podcasts online
And still that person you loved fucking died
Or they still broke your heart
Still cried at the lights
Still up on your Amex
Still down in your mind

Well I'm sorry, there's your apology
Now come on, there's still time
To step out of those shoes and into the light
Where you realise today isn't the sum of your life
Today's just a brick that makes up a house
It's more of a click than the whole big bang
And you'd feel so sick if the phone now rang
And heard your someone was in some crash
And they're too far gone and they're not coming back

You'd fall to your knees and kill anything
For twenty more minutes to hold them again
Well, it's kind of like that but you're the one driving
You're the one here with the chance to keep trying
And failing and laughing and hurting and crying
And making it matter for all this surviving
And making it worth it, the pain of this life
And you have two choices, I'll lay them out here;

Be hurt in love or be hurt in fear
That's the buy-in of life, it hurts while you're here
And you'll notice that those are receipts not tears
For the price you're paying to live sincerely

So I'm sorry for that thing that ruined your life
But it didn't, it just sort of fucked up your night
So find some good sleep and a comfortable bed
'Cos we're up in the morning, there's a long day ahead
And I know that you're thinking some wounds are too grave
And some graves are too deep to ever be saved

But I'll hold you to that when the birds stop singing
And if you're listening now then the phone's not ringing
So the crash so far must have not happened
And you're still just driving and not yet crashing
And it's in your hands so you choose what happens

I'm sorry for the thing that ruined your life
But the longer you let it, the sooner it might

In the elevator to heaven

Two billionaires were chatting
And one of them goes
'Ay, which penthouse are you getting?
'Cos I want the one that overlooks
The whole heavenly kingdom'

And the other said 'That's fine,
I plan to rule the garden'
And he could tell the first was jealous
That he hadn't thought of asking
His PA or his Mrs
To message God and ask him

So he said 'I was sorry to hear about the whole disaster
If it had been my plane that crashed, you'd have been flying faster
And you wouldn't have been trapped so long
In pain, in total darkness'

And the other guy said 'Ah it's cool,
I heard your death was fucked?
Shot outside your house in front of your wife?
That's kinda cucked'

And now this guy was seething
And the other guy as well
He said 'Get me outta this elevator,
'Cos right now this is hell'

And they both looked up in silence
Into some distant eyes
'How many floors to go?'
But God never replied

If nothing else

If there's one thing
To learn to do
It's walk into a room
Dressed in nothing but confidence

What men get wrong about women

They listen to men
(*On how to get women*)

Who listened to men
(*Failing with women*)

Who listened to men
(*Who only hurt women*)

Who listened to men
Who don't listen to women

I never thought about it but statistically
someone bought my book and died

And it's not impossible to say
That maybe if they hadn't
They would still be here now
Through some imperceptible nuance
Of butterfly behaviour

Didn't shower at 7:13am
Had a wank instead

Maybe 'Congratulations'
Was one of the ones they read
Missed the bus by two minutes
So on, so on, so forced
To live inside a merry-go-round
Where everything's alive

And had I never written it
Maybe they'd not sleep
And always always why must I
Make everything about me

There will be times when the world is too much

When the voltage is too high
For one hand to touch
And there will be times
When the world is unkind

Despite all your kindness
And doing things right

And there will be a moment
When you have to choose
If you love 'til you win
Or hurt 'til you lose

And sometimes you'll feel
That you're broken and done
And the only drawer left
Is the one with the gun

And too much was said
And you can't feel the sun
And if it was your funeral
No one would come

But what if today
We just listened for once
To the children we are
And our crying for love

And how you did not know
What the fuck to have done
When you woke up on Earth
With air in your lungs

And you did not know
What to make of all this
And if you made a mess –
Well, I bet you did

'Cos what else can you do
When you're learning to live

Maybe just always
That is what life is
Fucking it up
But not giving in

Doing it wrong
But learning something
Being in pain
While searching for bliss

And some days the pain is too much, yes it is
So we reach for the hands of those we would miss
If the world disappeared
And to them, you are this:

You are the world
Any time you exist
So yes, it's too much
That's definitely true

It hurts to give birth
And it hurts to live too
Every miracle hurts
And that's why you do

There will be times
When the world is too much
And there will be tomorrow
And you will be enough

I don't believe in presidents

But I still believe in people
I don't believe in the devil
But I have witnessed his evil

No, I don't believe in presidents
But I do believe in you
And when power wants you silent
We fight to speak the truth

When the TV wants you divided
We'll write our own news
Away from the illusion of
Good / bad, red or blue

It's the hardest pill to swallow
The fluidity of 'you'
And if you grew up somewhere different
Well, you'd be different too

And if your mother, father, friends, employer
Believed there was no moon
You'd stand under the midnight sky
Crying 'It's a ruse'

Nah, I don't believe in presidents
That's just a thing we do
In this pantomime reality
Where they let us pretend to choose

When actually the corporations
Print their profit 'truth'
To chip at and manipulate
Your spirit and your mood
And scare you into othering
Anyone but you
To keep you poor and terrified
Hidden in your room

So that anything they televise
It just becomes your view
Then wraps around your deepest fears
And digs into the bruise

They fund their favourite party
But make you buy the balloons
Then package it as freedom
And sell it back to you

So I don't believe in presidents
But I love you if you do
And as long as we remember that
The power lies with you

You're not in love, you're in pain

You're not obsessed 'cos it's unique or special
You're just traumatised
And absorbed the wrong message

Taught to fight for your value
To be proven and seen
But they're not that mysterious
They're actually just mean

If I could just get five minutes of not thinking about myself

I'd walk around the corner shop and neaten up the shelf
And check in on my neighbours, see if they needed any help
And swing by the police station, solve some cold cases as well
And actually read the article, not just skim the thing and tell
Everyone about something that I've just learnt myself
As if I'm suddenly enlightened and they need to check themselves

If I could just get one quick second, just to think of someone else
And how they wish their daughter hadn't died
And miss the way she smelled
And how they might be sort of thirsty from this vivid sense of hell

I'd offer my condolences, let them scream into my mouth
I'd swallow all their suffering and tidy up their house
And cook them up some homemade thing
And give them shit as well
Because kindness isn't niceness and love always prevails
No, it's not okay to rot away and isolate yourself
Someone out there needs you to neaten up their shelf

Then I'd snap out of this daydream
Open up my phone (my cell!)
And post this little poem
And congratulate myself

If I could get five minutes
Of not thinking about myself
I'd wonder what you're thinking
Do you think of me as well

If he loved you, he would

And you wouldn't have to ask
That's a thing we like to say
Before we break our own hearts

And 'If you knew me, you'd just do it'
Because love is telepathic
Even though half the shit I do
And say is mostly automatic

I barely understand myself
But expect you to! Just classic
I don't know why I'm in this awful mood
But if you loved me you'd just crack it

And adjust yourself to serve my thoughts
And my emotional palette

Never stopping to observe
That my head is where life happens
You're crying on some sinking ship
But brother, you're the captain

You can't stand there like some party guest
Watching glasses as they shatter
Then blame the water and the waves
When you're the one who's crashing

And some of us have fragile hearts
And pasts that hold us captive
And scars in fonts a knife would write
'Love with care' on our wrappers

But all of us must make our peace
And that journey is your duty
If you use the love you learned in hate
You'll punish all the beauty

And it isn't that romantic
And it isn't very chic
But the only way they'll love you right
Is to ask for what you need

I'd never be a Nazi

'Cos me, I am not evil
I just want to live in peace
And always protect people

I could not be brainwashed
No matter how scared I get
Though the way the world is going, man
There's not much to protect
What Grandad built with his bare hands
There's almost nothing left
They're coming for our culture
They want us to forget

I'd watch out for these immigrants
They're planning something big, I bet

You watch, they'll show up in our schools
Get in your children's head
But I'd never be a Nazi
No, I just want what's best

I used to volunteer at the food bank
And my God, what a mess
They're handing out these meals
To the scum – aren't we in debt?

It's you and me, the taxpayer
We're their safety net
And I was listening to this podcast
Did you get the link I sent?

This guy man, he just gets it
He says we should take the power back
If we cared about our wives and kids
We'd prepare for their attack

So I volunteered at the detainment centre
Just tryna do my bit
'Cos I look into my daughter's eyes
And she's got so much life to live

I just want her to be safe
Have all the freedom that we did
And God, if we don't stop this hate
Ahh man, it makes me sick

So I'm happy to be here
This is my second shift
I'll help you round them up
After I finish this cig

And there isn't that much to it
Just watch out for the kids
Sometimes the handcuffs slip
'Cos they're too big for their wrists

But eventually they'll fall in line
And it's the strangest thing
If you break 'em down hard enough
They'll walk themselves right in

And when you shut the chamber door
Sometimes they start to sing
Or pray to their demonic God
You know, that kind of thing

And some of our lads were throwing up
But trying their best to hide it
The embarrassment of seeming weak
No good man can survive it

But I got home to my daughter
And God, sometimes she's stupid
I said 'Love, I'd never be a Nazi'
And she said 'Fucking prove it'

Today

I saw a woman with her hand in the back pocket of her man's jeans
And maybe it's the music playing as I write this from a car
Passing through this city I had to kill myself to dream in
High on the endorphins of the majesty I'm feeling
But how do you all do it, how do you cope with the wonder

A man taking a photo of his white dress wife
On Shaftesbury Avenue
The smell of caramel and grey-blue England over St James's Park
The neon red and blue in all of us and you
How do you survive it, the endlessness of beauty

I refuse to believe it, the postmodern lie
That nothing here matters – is the clue not that you die
Is the meaning and the magic not so clearly in the eyes
Of this boy outside The Old Vic with his dad by his side

Have you not heard the music or seen the film and cried
Today – and you – this feeling
I hope it lasts the night

Has anyone checked on the boys?

'Cos if it's 2am and the text comes in
Saying 'I love you man, thanks for everything'
You would fight, crash, fly, drive, murder and swim
All through the night just to get to him

But we miss all the moments before it's fever pitch
The gradual isolation and the daily slip
Another inch down the mountain 'til he's at the cliff
Staring over the edge, challenging the abyss
And as much as we'll punish ourselves over this
And ruminate on ways we could have changed something

If I'd just made time, or just checked in
Or stayed for dinner, played PlayStation
Told him I loved him then told him again
Maybe we wouldn't have lost a friend

But life is a private thing we witness
And if the mind's too tired it's unable to listen
No, wait, not tired – that word dismisses
The truth of the matter, and the matter is this:

It's not a lack of sleep, it's a lack in the value
Of self-perception, not seeing the man who
We all adore and want to see more of
Who feels the love we're all so sure of

And the joy he brings to the world around him
So maybe yes, if at the cliff you found him

You could've saved him once, that's fair
And in that moment show you care
But then he'll have to search for himself
And breathe and breathe and love far inward
When you check on the boys
Guess who to begin with

Like when a plane starts crashing
You have to save yourself first
Sometimes checking on the boys
Is to admit I'm hurting

Maybe you didn't give up on your dreams

Maybe they were the dreams of a seven-year-old
Or terrified parents
Or a life in a film you saw one night
In the summer holiday

When everything was closer
And safely impossible
When it cost you nothing to dream of it
Maybe they were the dreams
Of a child who just wanted love
And misspelled it 'attention'

Maybe you just wanted to be impressive
'Cos then you'd feel safe and valued and welcome

Like shopping for clothes online
Maybe those dreams fit better in your head
And when you tried them on
You felt less like yourself

But the miracle thing about dreaming is
Every night you can dream again
And nothing that's yours
Can ever be taken

The person you are is an estimation
Whatever your plans, you're only just guessing
And hating yourself for betraying your betting
Will only keep you asleep in depression

See look now I'm rhyming
That wasn't the plan
Tried to write one that was looser than that
But life always takes you
Where it needs you

And you're standing here
Like no one sees you
Like someone out there has not just dreamed you
Waiting for you to wake, all asleep
Didn't get what you want
But you'll get what you need

'Cos the death of a dream tastes like rejection
But one day you'll see it was always protection

Good people

Do not bend over backwards
To stay in the good books
Of bad people

I had a message saying 'You saved my life'

But it wasn't me, I'm not that nice
I just mumble, speak and write
You're the one who put down the knife
Stepped off the bridge, declined the light
At the end of the tunnel, returned to life

To start again, survived the night
Hello, good morning, fuckin' right
Off we go, all in attendance
Take a breath for those who left us

Those who didn't make the day
And I don't care if it's cliche
All of this was just to say
I'm glad you're here
I hope you stay

An unexpected consequence of healing

Enjoying your favourite films / music
Less than ever
Because the hurt within you
No longer resonates

The pain receptors not firing
No reaction, stand down soldier
War's over, dried blood in poppy fields

No one prepares you
For the beautiful dullness
Of being okay
'Cos you thought 'feeling'
Was being in pain

Nothing hurts more than the joy of a woman

You will notice this trend
In boys who aren't men
Who sleep with a girl
Then tell all their friends

How awful she was
Or how much she loved it
All snarling and proud
Like killing for justice

For all of the girls
Who never text back
Ignored him in school
Or chose to unmatch

He'll punish this one
For confirming his fear
That you'd have to be broken
To ever come near him

This twisted inverted
Disturbing perception
That she is the enemy
Sex is the weapon

She is the glory
He won't learn his lesson
She'll headline the story
And time will forget him

Made it, made what

He woke up at 16
Then woke up at uni
Then woke up with strangers
Then broke up on Brook Street

Slept for most his twenties
Reading, Leeds & ket dreams
Clocked in at the office
Thinking 'Hope I can forget me'

Then he bought a load of stuff
Like some trainers and some sun
Too busy making something
Of himself to make his lunch

Forgot the miracle of strangers
And forgot to call his mum
And forgot to have some children
'Cos he forgot to meet their mum

And he blinked awake at 40
Bored of everything he's got
Made it all the way to 90
He said 'Made it?
Made what?'

One last bomb for freedom

They stand in the war room
All sweating, ties loosened
A hundred boxes
Of take-out noodles

He's shaking and naked
With blood on his tongue

Crying 'Come on, pleeease
Just ONE last bomb'

He asked me to write this before his girl dies

In 37 days – 36 when I wrote this
Eight hundred and sixty hours
That's a cruel prognosis
If you live in a body and time is your captor

But the beauty of a soul is, the body's just the wrapper
The body's just the packaging of infinite light
That loves and illuminates all through your eyes
In every other life he'd make you his wife
But if it's just this one, then good, that's right
'Cos I'll tell you where love goes after it dies
Absolutely fucking nowhere, it stays by your side
And we carry it with us it glows so bright
It can feel like a burn, but it's not, here's why

'Cos if you look real close there's a miracle in it
Be it 36 days or 36 minutes
If you let it all in, love closes the distance
Between time zones and planes of existence
In fact, my God, that's the thing we're missing
Love after death, that's just long-distance

In 37 days, the sun will set
That's a war cry to my ears – we're not done yet
That's one for anger and one to resent
And one for sympathy and one to repent
And one to forgive and none to forget
And by my maths that's still 32 left
To love and hold and gracefully listen
To all those around you preparing to miss you

I can wrap it up pretty in a poem
And I'm touched to
But your boy just wants you to know
That he loves you

My therapist said if you have depression and

Watch porn
Watch the news
Scroll through the 'for you'
Kissed that person that time
But your girl never knew

Finally landed the job
Of your parents' dreams
Studied for years for their chosen degree
Minimised all of your baseline needs
And had six months of five hours sleep

Then said 'no' to that homeless woman
Needing three pounds for tampons
Then bought that cocktail
That cost twelve pounds and
Went looking for love
But kept things casual

'Cos it's more fun to do
When there's so much to choose
But there's nothing to win
If there's nothing to lose

Said if all of that stuff sounds like you
There's a very good chance
You might find this rude

But if your life is a nightclub
You shout over the noise of
You're not depressed, you're hungover
From all of the poison

I had a comment the other day

Saying 'Shut up you cunt'
Then underneath that 'I love this so much'
Then one after that said 'Bro this ain't tuff'
Then someone sent a tattoo pic of my stuff
Inked on their arm, you'd think that'd be enough

To solidify the validity of whatever I've done
Then someone pointed out my beard's ginger in the sun
And I should go and kill myself
And ahh it's all fun

But then I had a message from this dead boy's Mum
Saying she's sorting out his funeral (cause the ideation won)
Thinks her heart's no longer beating 'cos her greatest love is gone

And she couldn't find the words quite precise enough in song
So she asked to read my poem about 'No Flowers' – that one

She said 'Can I read it at the funeral?'
I said 'Do anything you want
Lie down on the carpet and scream until the font
In the label on the rug
Starts to bleed into the mud
Until you summon up the dead
Until your boy returns and haunts
You beautifully, lovingly, perpetually
And flaunts his spirit through your house'

That's what I'd have fucking done
If I lost my only boy, wouldn't even ask someone
For permission to read 'Good News'
If anybody knows that one

Ahh I don't expect you to know it
If it wasn't written for you
But sometimes what you hate
Saves the people who won't call you

When the darkness gets too dark
And the laughter's just a mask

And all of you who make shit
It's a pretty noble duty
To look into a page or camera
Awaiting hate and scrutiny
And still, you do it anyway
'Cos someone might wake up as usual
Then suddenly get the news today
They need to plan a funeral

And they need to pick the music
And they have nothing to read
And they don't think they can do it
Then they see you on their screen
And God knows why it's moving

But it wraps them up in feathers
And takes the weight from off their chest
The world gets slightly better

'Cos everything you've ever seen
That made you wanna cry
Or motivated, educated, helped you stay alive
Was dreamt up by a person
Who half the time missed

And if you're laughing at the wrapping paper
You won't get the gift

So you can burn all of your words
And live a life of quiet
Think 'Now I won't be criticised !
Now I'm safe from violence !'

But you'll be at the funeral
And have nothing to read
And goodness dies in silence
So I think you should speak

You do not have to say the right thing

Or know who you are
Or know how to act
Be the life of the party
Or any of that

You just need to be
Awake and alive
It's too easy to feel
You're wasting your life

Or worry on worry
About getting it right
Well why be so easy?
It's much harder to fight

For the beauty in balance
And accepting a life
Where you were in pain
Then you were alright
It was good, it was bad
Then you wanted to die

Yeah, it rains on your wedding
But love doesn't mind
And maybe you're 7 or 75
But wherever you're heading
You'll get there on time

Whenever you're dancing
You're doing it right
Whenever you're laughing
Or dreaming or crying

No, you do not have to say the right thing
You just have to mean it
It's your song to sing

'Cos sometimes you're out
And sometimes you're in
And you'll think it's all over
And then it begins

This country is an abusive parent

And this is what we don't understand about war
Our outrage is already accounted for
When our leaders drop bombs on anyone's land
Our anger was budgeted as part of the plan

'Cos to us, in our houses and jobs
On our streets, where we chat about weather
Put the bin out each week

To us, we think 'You'd have to be crazy
To not feel bad about killing these babies'
But our governments look back at us with straight faces
Turns your blood cold
When you learn what this place is

All of this land we call a country or nation
This red, white and blue identification
Is not the hero on a mission to save us
It's just a business where profit needs making
And bullets are cheap and need constant replacing
So the war keeps flowing and their champagne chases

We are just children abused by our parents
We can march all we want screaming 'Take care of us'
But that's the confusion they've dazzled us with
Thinking our wants mean anything

We're kids in the garden
Shouting at the house
With our dad drunk on power
Stumbling about
Smashing up glasses and people we love
Then telling us softly
'I did this for us'

Drop the slave name

No no no, Jones is my name boy
Got children and agents of love
Under that name boy
Got beautiful black curly curls
And Taliah Waajid curl cream
In that hair boy

Got bank accounts
Books and trust funds
In that name boy
And no trace left
Of your name boy
Forgotten, rescinded
Unwritten here boy

My family tree starts
At Dad's dad, boy
Or his dad's dad
Can't find you boy

Can't bury or buy back
Your soul boy
Can't see you or save you
Or name you boy

And here is the final
Moment in your history
The end of you boy
And you are forgiven

Man's only enslaved
To his anger boy
And I release you
Be gone now, boy

I still believe in love

Like I still believe in Christmas
And maybe all the miracle
Comes from what you're wishing

It comes from what you choose to say
And maybe wish you didn't
To find a way to keep your heart
When you've been falsely imprisoned

In a world that wants you cold and numb
Afraid of being different
I still believe in you and us
No matter what the distance

Billionaire internet boys' club

And it's funny
These masculine things
They've done

When I look at these men
I can't see <u>one</u>

The beautiful thing about dying is this:

The moment we're born
We must one day be missed
By those who carried us through this existence

And look, I don't know what the reason is
But I sometimes think it might be this:

That time is for us to measure the days
Time is kind of just something we say
Time is just 'Hi, yeah, I'll see you at eight'
But time is not for the souls gone away

For them, the time has no name
It's always forever, it's always today
And if we remember that we'll find a way
To speak them into each word we say

When infinity feels like the pain of today
When losing one so precious and brave
A soul too innocent to ever have stayed
So they hurried ahead and there they will wait

When after this life, at the end of the play
When the curtain rolls back, you walk off the stage
And the living will cry and clap and wave
As you safely return to wherever we're made

You'll laugh at the list of the things you prayed
And how silly and human it was this game
Where you could not feel or find your place
As a soul in a world of glass and plates
Trivial things we hold and break

'Cos the beautiful thing about dying is this:
The price of entry – is you have to exist

Know this:

You are who you decide to be
Not who you were once

Don't tell the children

But they're completely right
We don't know a fucking thing
About living this life

You're not *more* of a human
'Cos your face is more straight
The kids knew all along
We were put here to play

The relationship's dead, where do we hide the body?

You already know
No, it's already done
You might laugh with each other
Might even be fun
But that fire that once
Made jealous the sun
After all these years
Couldn't warm anyone

You already know
See, destiny won
You lie with each other
Like a hand on a gun
And you lie to each other
That the morning won't come

But sometimes I love you
Sounds like 'I release you'
And nothing like hatred
Said only to keep you

From missing your life
And the peace you've been chasing
You won't see it now
But one day you'll be grateful

That one of you found the strength
Though it's painful
I can't let you drown
In the romance of rainfall

No matter how pretty the petrichor
Dangerous to burn with the house
Or go down with the ship
Or whatever your preferred metaphor is

'Cos one day somewhere
You'll be at a train station
And know you must leave
But find yourself waiting

And your heart will bleed
As they say 'I'll miss you'
But love never once
Held anyone prisoner

It's fear that traps
And suffers and chains
And the grief only hurts
When the love remains

Where do we hide the body
When the relationship dies?
We don't, we say 'Thank you,
Have a beautiful life'

The deradicalisation of a 21st-century man

I think I am balanced
And do not have a Flat Earth
I think I am fair and kind
Would not cause any hurt

I would not drop the bomb
I would not be a killer
I would stop the bad guy
And not dance at his party

And to stop him
If I had to
I would probably kill him
But I would not enjoy it
Or find that at all fulfilling

I am on the right side
Of a beautiful bright history
Where goodness stands on grass so green
And everyone will miss me

I do not trust the media
I am not easily led
I decided for myself
The clothes in which I'm dressed

I had the choice of trousers
Or slightly shorter trousers
I have the choice of being burned
Or buried but with flowers

I'd abolish slavery
And boycott cotton sales
And post about the boycott
On my child labour cell

I would not fund the cartel
Or sex trafficking they sell
And yes my week was hard
But this cocaine is for myself

'Cos a dog is man's best friend
And when mine died I cried
So all my friends, they took me out
For pig and bird and fries
And as we ate the burning flesh
Took photos on the phone
Did lines under the desk
Watched porn when I got home

Paid tax towards the bombs
I felt something was wrong
I scrolled until I'd scrolled
And then I put my finger on it:

I pictured all the bad guys
Sitting with their kids
And feeling they'd kill anyone
Who ever threatened this

I pictured all the villains
With nailed coffin lids
And all their family crying tears
And singing 'He'll be missed'

I pictured just a man somewhere
Getting his trousers fixed
Thought if it comes down to me or him
I know which one I'd pick

And I realised not a man or woman
Ever to have lived
Has ever felt the problem
Was anything they did

I saw God on the train

But pretended I didn't
So I sat far away from the seat he was sitting in
And then he got up, I think probably to piss
And he noticed me there and said 'Oi oi, what's this?

What you saying? Are you hiding from me?'
I said 'Ahh mate nah, just a comfier seat'
And he looked at me like I was a kid covered in chocolate
Surrounded by wrappers, saying 'Don't know what happened'

And he goes 'Come on then mate, I've got a few minutes
Tell me what's wrong but don't fuck around with it'
And it shocked me then that it fit in one sentence
I said 'I just think heaven's a stupid incentive

Like what, a shit life for a beautiful death?
And those who are evil, can suddenly repent
Like a killer or nonce can live like a monster
Then right at the end say "I'm sorry, dear God sir"
And end up in Heaven, right there with my nana
She's doing some knitting, he's waving a hammer

It's like Jesus, God what a horrible deal'
And he goes 'Yeah it's fucked, I know how you feel'
I'm like 'Mate, you're the one spinning the wheel'

And God goes 'Listen, I'll tell you a secret
All of that stuff, mate I didn't speak it
Like the old joke says about liars and men:
"If God wrote the book – why are you holding the pen?"
Nah, the rules I wrote, I wrote on your heart

The truth I spoke you've known from the start
Be kind and don't harm – it isn't that hard
Heaven's just life if you're doing your part
You want white clouds and endless skies?
Err yeah, look around, you don't have to die

I know it probably brings you some pain
To think of the dead as just dust in a grave
But humans can't comprehend it when I say
Life is the cloud and death is the rain'

And I got to my stop and felt kinda mad
I'm not sure he answered the questions I had
And then I looked up and saw the sun rising
He said 'You're looking for heaven
But you're the one hiding'

Your boy's last compliment

Was in 2012
He was sitting at McDonald's
Not talking to the girls
And the pretty one from the year above
Said 'What's that fucking smell?'

And she sniffed around the boys
You were there as well
And she stopped at him, eyes squinted
He thought 'Oh fucking hell'

Preparing to get cut to shreds
Embarrassed of himself
But she goes 'No I'm serious
Your shirt smells really nice'

And he didn't know what to say
So he said 'Thank you'
He thanked her twice

And no one else up to that point
Had said something so nice
And he sat there in the booth
Until his Coke was all just ice

And off she went, into the world
Into a beautiful night
And off he went back to his room
And it probably saved his life

The man who died at his desk job

I can't think of his name
But you know the one – the guy
Think his trousers were dark grey

Well anyway me and him
Used to take our lunch together
And one day, it was raining
We said in unison 'This weather...'

And did that closed mouth smile
That you do at stranger-friends
But little did he know
This is where his story ends

And right before he vanished
Back into the ether
He looked at me in tears
Said 'Was I a good team leader?'

I looked at him all serious
Said 'Stay with us, we need ya'
Then I ran into him in heaven
And we shared a frozen pizza

And we reminisced about old reports
And colleagues (fuck you, Peter)
And we looked down from the clouds
New faces, office desk, four-seater

He said 'I never did get through the work'
And I said 'Yeah, me neither'

You can't be a victim forever

If I shout at you 'cos you're not listening
Then you hit me, I am the victim

If I hit you back
You'd say we're even
If you hit me harder
Now we're fighting

If I hit you harder
It's a war
If I hit you hardest
It's a war crime

If I hit you always
All your children
All your schools
Hospitals burning

Strip you of your place of worship
Eviscerate and straight up murder

Then I can't say I'm still the victim
'Cos I'm still here
And you are missing

Me / ADHD

Woke up, scrolled through my daily diagnosis of BPD
Bi-polar autism and acute C-PTSD and finally defined
My very niche sexual orientation as
'Neo-Hetero-AFAB presenting women preferring'
And just tap water is fine please, and I finally worked out that my
Late onset
Dissociative abandonment attachment style
Was maladaptive to my HDMI connecting an old VHS to watch
My own home videos
And dissect my fragile narcissism
And pinpoint the exact moment my pure-O OCD became full
    blown intrusive suicidal ideation and how that might explain
My tendency to lie in bed and procrastinate, there's no other
Explanation

There's no other way to find meaning
Now that all the meaning is gone
The youth centres are shut, the music venues closing down
So I am this and I am that
What else is there to be
Who is left to be a fan of
Other than my own personality and neurology
God's dead so there are bigger mysteries at hand here
Like why don't I like the feeling of sand on my feet at the beach
Is that my hyper-sensitivity auto-didact tryptophobia
Diet Coke and smoke aroma incense sage from Nova Scotia

Ex-boyfriend and girlfriend claim
Both to have been gaslit, someone here's lying
But no one will admit it

Traumatised and trauma bonding
Holding hands with all of you
'Cos in this limbo end of times
There's nothing else to fucking do

It's the house with the balloons out front

And I know it's weird to have balloons at a funeral
But balloons at a birthday are just as unusual
A symbol of life contained in a skin
And one little prick can fuck the whole thing

So there's balloons out front and she's filled them with grief
Blown out of her lungs and her breath tastes sweet
When she opens the door and it's such a weird scene

She's eating some Haribo from a table of treats
And everyone's there, the whole family
Think that's the thing about PTSD
Everyone's frozen, expecting the police
To burst through the door, all trapped in a dream

And I say, half-joking, that balloon isn't floating
And point to her heart, she says 'That one's broken
But I keep blowing out air, still hoping'
And that's the best a mother can do

When her daughter's boyfriend's face on the news
Stares into your house, this monster who
Once sat around and helped cook food
And spoke politely, spent birthdays too

Is now in prison and barely at that
'Cos it's hard to prove intent in black and white
So he just got 'manslaughter'
This man who slaughtered someone's daughter

Oh wow, that's nice, just sentenced to eight
He'll probably do four – that's light, that's great
And he'll come out and head to the pub
And celebrate life and still be loved
By all of his boys and mum and stuff
Will sort of carry on as usual

Best not mention anything brutal
Just 'I don't think he meant to kill her'
'I just think he has a temper'
But that boy there's a fucking killer
They live among us, dressed for dinner

And we're tidying up, popping balloons with pins
And she hesitates to stab it in
This beautiful soul under beautiful skin
And this one little prick took everything

Doing okay checklist

Did you get out of bed?
Did you brush your teeth?
Did you choose to live?
Did you manage to eat?

If you did none of these
Did you manage to sleep?
If you couldn't do that
Did you think at least?

Okay you had thoughts?
Well they're no different to dreams
That's a light in the distance
And that's all you need

Success isn't scaling a mountain
Or cash
It's what you can manage
At the minimal amount

Until you can handle what's just out of reach
And that, that and that, 'til you set yourself free

And all of that chat
Is just really to say
Wherever you're at
You're doing okay

Love is a house that you build by the beach

If it's left unprotected
It's lost to the sea

But before all the wreckage
It starts with a leak
Some tangled resentment
Or fragility

That will poison your thinking
You'll say shit you don't mean
All jealous of someone your someone
Might meet

And hasn't ! but could !
And didn't ! but might !
And oh God I love you
Please don't wreck my life

Love is a house you build over time
We build it together
Then leave it behind

Activist [in bio]

I have not been arrested
Or even been pestered
I've argued with no one
But Dad and his guest list
At whatever party I'm already at

I have not turned up
Sat in or boycotted
I cancelled the author
I love Harry Potter

I take none of the risk
But all of the glory
I know not the names
Of my comrades before me

I sip on a coffee
The wind in my hair
I take all your fears
And make myself scared

Then claim that the cause
Is personal, yeah
I am at the protest
But just for the photo

There's no place like home
In Kansas, Toto

An artist is a hunter

sorry to disappoint
but inspiration doesn't come

doesn't slump at your feet
and surrender 'you've won'

inspiration is a beast
first and fastest to run

you're waiting to be chased
but honey you're the gun

End Paragraph

All along the mess we were making, a hundred fireworks all at once, paint on your hands, sugar on your teeth, blood pumping, running, running, fucking, always somewhere – never here, and dreaming, looking as far and forever as we could into the whitest light you've ever seen, never alone, haunted alone, loneliest girl in the city alone, a forest fire at the edge of paradise, young, getting younger, a million birthday candles, crying at the magic

Or just some girl having a nosebleed in a flat in Hackney Wick

I'll always be raining

At parties and weddings
In tuxedos and in the middle
Of the TV series
In bed or at beaches

Where red dresses and clutch bags
And cameras are flashing
I'll always be raining

When laughing and playing
When younger and 20, sorry
I'm not really listening

When stood in town freezing
With girls in their heels
And not really hearing
Or here or healed

And I'll still see the sun
Though its beauty is painful
But some way, somehow
I'll always be raining

Me if I die before my girl

Her: *screaming* how are you back

Me: sorry babe forgot something

Me: *little forehead kiss*

Me: alright cool, see you later, take your time, I'll wait

Have you heard the story of the Wolf and the Beach?

It's this thing I found written in a diary in a loft
It was wrapped in a cloth and locked in a box
The cover said 'If you find this, please do not
Open it. Please.' It said 'Keep this lost'
And I wondered if I should
But ahh why not

And the first page said
'Beware of the wolf
Who lives in the trees
Beware of the wolf
Who waits 'til you sleep

Beware of the wolf
Who swims in the sea
Wolf wants you dead
Wolf wants our Beach

Wolf haunts our land
The dog of the devil
The Beach is ours
We built this Heaven'

And then some pages had been ripped
And torn away, the story clipped and rearranged

Someone must have been enraged
Or wanted something kept away
Something someone should not say
And the book itself had no date

It skipped straight to this distant page
Said 'Wolf is dead, God heard us pray
Wolf is burned, his cubs our slaves
And all the Beach will celebrate
Today is now Beach Freedom Day

And every year, we'll build a pyre
Burn an effigy, Wolf on fire
And all the Beach will live forever
Happy, safe, in love together'

And I just could not let it go
Like, what was ripped and missing though?
What was taken from the story
How was Wolf defeated, surely

Someone, somewhere must be proud
Of ending Wolf and evil, how?

So I went searching, looked for years
Through all these boxes, locked in fear
'Til I found these pages
Stained with tears

Wrapped in a cloth of blood
It was weird
Like something / someone disappeared
They said 'If you find this, don't be scared
Please be brave & please forgive
Do not do what we all did
Life is all we have to live'

And in these pages, lay the truth
Man I was shaking, so confused
The chapter was titled: 'Before the Wolf'

'There was a beach
With cubs and pups, she-wolves in peace
Where life was lived and dreamt in sleep
Where Wolf would dance and play and dream

Then we arrived, came from the sea
Wolf was smiling – but we saw teeth
We scorched the coast, killed the beast
Took the cubs as ours to keep
Chained them, named them, set them free
From Wolf and all his tyranny

Some Wolf escaped, into the woods
And now Wolf threatens all that's good
See Wolf just wants to steal our peace
And we won't stop 'til Wolf's defeated'

And I took the pages to the police
Wrote the government, wrote the leaders
And they said 'Thank you, we'll take these
Now you take care, enjoy the Beach'

**No matter what you buy,
you're only ever renting**

Everything's on credit
No matter how you spend it

And we should hold it gently
And gratefully and tight

You only own a home
As much as you own light

You can wear the clothes
But only for tonight

For anyone thinking 'I'll never love again'

I know you think you won't find another them
But you also believed that you'd always be friends
With the kids on your street when you were like ten
So ah, there's no reason to worry about that

What do you know, your whole life's just a blag
Yeah, your heart's all broken and tattered and cracked
You forgot who you are – I promise you'll be back
Yeah, it feels like you're dying, but try to relax
Just feel all the grief and the panic attacks
And let them subside of their own volition

And try to forgive, fuck, that's the mission
That's the part that will free you of decades
Of bitter resentment and texts you'll send them
Like 'You ruined my life'
Instead, think 'Bless them'
They were just trying and young and guessing
Probably weren't aiming for all this depression

No, thank them instead for this valuable lesson
What else can you do with the rage in your heart
Than tear it all up, think 'What was my part?
What did I do? Who will I be now?'
I'm starting brand new, I'm working out how
To frame it in love then burn it all down
As a gift to the wind – what a beautiful sound

I know you think you won't find another them
Well you won't, that's the point
This cycle must end
Not all broken branches are meant to be nests
Yeah, your life is over, now go live the rest

So for anyone thinking I'll never love again
It starts with yourself
Actually, that's where it ends

The King of Therapy

You know how your therapist needs a therapist
That little fact you hear at parties
And on the fourth slide of a @therapy.memes post
Well I want that motherfucker

I want the guy who
My therapist's therapist's therapist
Has to go and see, the big dog
King Therapist, sitting in the most peaceful
Padded mid-century English room

I wanna walk in and see my guy dressed on some wizard shit
I wanna hear him say 'Enter, child'
Sitting all creeked out in a corner
I wanna see his eyebrow muscles twisted into a permanent frown
From decades and decades of listening to veteran therapists
Talking about the worst worst worst words
You could possibly hear

I wanna sit opposite that guy and say
'I offer my broken self to you for repair, sir'
And I want him to say something so impossibly profound
So celestial and eternally true
That the hairs on my neck and arms stand permanently for life

I wanna leave the room in tears, screaming,
Running down the corridor
Crying thank you, thank you, oh fuck help, thank you
And just then, as I run out into oncoming traffic,
Healed and brand new
I want the King of Therapy to open a secret hatch
Beneath his office desk

I want him to descend into a long-forgotten vault of a room
Knock on a blood red door and say 'Master, the time has come'
'Witness me, my master'
As he kneels before the final_final_FINAL_therapist.wav

And I dread to think beyond that
And I dread to think, beyond that

Someone said I never criticise women

And I only write about the men who kill 'em
And I kind of feel like that's kind of a given
But actually, fair, there's some stuff I'm missing
And I don't wanna get all what-about-ism

'Cos yeah, light splits when it's viewed through a prism
And maybe my views aren't full definition
I'm biased and based and my viewership listens
To whatever ideas they're already riffing

So yeah
I guess women do bad stuff too
And shit I don't know, I don't wanna be rude
But ain't it our job to be sharp on the truth?
So here's a critique of the bad women do:

My observations, hmm, what can I use?
Okay yeah, I think a unique kind of cruel
Is when women are threatened by women they will
Assassinate secretly that woman whilst all saying

'Oh my God babe, I love that dress'
Then say something brutal the moment she's left

That's a thing I think, it's not really a good one
I guess maybe women could uplift more women
But ahh that's more about pressure on beauty
And youth and a consequence of duty

Being forced to compete in a rigged election
Where men share power based on erections
And as soon as it drops, he'll slash her value
But hang on, oh shit, I'm back to men, whoa

Okay again, let's try a new set
Yeah, I guess some women do weaponise sex
Especially if they're tryna get back at an ex
But then I don't know, I guess so do men
They're just matching the score for gaslighting them

Nah fuck that, wait
I can criticise women
Just give me a second, it'll work in a minute
Sorry, fuck, this never happens
Just need a moment, I'm nervous, embarrassed

Like mate what do you want me to say
Women can be abusers too, great
Definitely yes, that's true and the truth
Women can bully and kill and be awful
And should be in prison when being unlawful

So okay yeah, women are women
And bad people can live within 'em
But when I say 'men' I don't mean MAN
I mean nested behaviours that are taught to him
When no real man has taught him better

And the same is true for women, oh yessir
But this is the mess of the word 'patriarchy'
It's not your mate all scared at a party
Who's kind and sweet and would like a Mrs
Wants to treat her kindly and enjoy her kisses

It's more of a background noise in the world
Whispered in boardrooms, preying on girls
A culture of power that makes you complicit
Fighting for scraps to spit on your spirit

But I guess if I had to criticise women
I would say this – if they choose to listen
Be careful that all of the hurt from men
Does not turn you into men
And make you hate
What's soft and femme
I think . . . but maybe then again
Lots of women are masculine

Fuckin' hatred makes you hate yourself
Quiet, lost and disrespected
Hate anything where you're reflected

I saw a girl in a coffee shop once
Buying a sandwich, I think for her lunch
And the guy at the till said 'That's a big meal
For a girl like you!' and gave her the bill

And she looked shattered, pale and ill
And I can't imagine how that shit feels
And you've seen boys crushing up pills
Dusting her drink against her will

So I could stand and criticise women
But I'd rather spend my breath on living a life
Where boys wake up in their life
Not with shame or misery in it
But joy enough to share and to give it

Freely and proudly, peacefully, loudly

Where love is not some skin to sleep on
And not just nudes to keep and leak on
Whatever chat when you're rejected
A man of honour is a man perfected

So yeah, I don't know, I don't care if I'm honest
But I care about caring, that's a promise

There's a man, there's a girl
There's a church, there's a steeple
Don't care about women
Care about people

Dating in the city:

We went for dinner and I was weird

Angel mum

I know you're angry
And yes you're allowed
That anger is yours, you carry it proud
Like the diamond your future collapsed around

And you probably won't even hear it right now
If I told you a soul is an infinite sound
But you don't want to hear about angels and clouds
You want to stay inside your house

And burn all the baby books you found
On the internet and hand-me-downs
You don't wanna speak, you sleep on the couch
You don't wanna eat or open your mouth

'Cos your voice would've been their favourite sound
And it's all too much to think of now
And if there's a God, please tell me how
And where the fuck is all His power

Yeah, He did the flood? Do the baby shower
Was it a day of rest? Some sacred hour?
Is He sorry yet? Is He sending flowers?

Then the anger decays to hollow grief
Gets in your bones, it aches in your teeth
But the beautiful thing about children is
In any form that they exist
Your love for them is still the gift

Their love for you transcends the rift
It drums the pulse inside your wrist
Your bleeding heart is where they live
And you keeping love alive is it
That's all we ever have to give

'Cos God is just a word sometimes
'Love' and 'Goodness' are better rhymes
And the irony is pantomime
'Cos God's so clear in a child's eyes

So we must live how we would raise a child
When you're ready, take your time

The world will be here when you need it
And always, when you cannot feel it
There is still goodness and yes you're needed
To carry love

To keep believing

[A Hug After That Sad Poem]

The kind you see on TV
Some big bright red
And blush pink roses
Awaiting at your feet

As you arrive home from a walk
Or back from overseas
All autumn brown & Christmas kissed
And naked as the trees

Curled up fox-like in your bed
You softly fall asleep
And all tomorrow waits for you
You have everything you need

I might not get there with you

But I'll leave everything I can
I'll write it all in black and white
To remind you who I am

Voting Day

I'm dancing with ghosts
I'm casting the vote
I'm laughing in Pret
Whilst kids are in boats
And drowning pursuing a flicker of hope
Oh that's not an ocean, oh no that's a moat
Built by the kings of this castle, whoa
There's a witch in the water but the body won't float
'Cos all superstitions stem from the throne
Our beliefs about self and what's 'our own'
It's all just stuff some matey just wrote

If somebody told you aged ten in your home
A man lives in the loft and he's judging your soul
Based on how obedient, polite and controlled
You promised to be, but he loves you, no
He'll just punish you bad if you step out of line
And send you to burn in infinite fire
And you mustn't kiss men, give him half of your rent
To ensure that he looks after you when you're dead
If I told you that thing again and again
At a time when your brain was forming and ten

You'd say that you 'knew' this thing you'd been told
And defend it to the death when you're 40 years old
But what do we know that we really can know
Can't even prove I'm awake or woke

Like maybe our ancestors just killed the most
And taught us to toast whilst they hung them from ropes
And thanked them all for their stolen coasts
And ravaged their farms for some pretty coats
And then wonder why their kids can't cope
When the weapons we sold that destroyed their homes
Still scorch the skies and shatter their bones
I'm singing head, shoulders, knees and toes
While they're learning their bloodline no longer flows
Their family tree now stands alone

How far does the love of a politician go
As far as his wallet, haha nah I joke
It's shorter than that, it stops at his nose
It stops where we say it does
Stops when your soul

Realises, fuck
My whole life is a vote

Who told you that love was easy?

Children come crying born into this life
Mothers in pain, sometimes under the knife
Who told you that you don't have to bleed
To heal the cuts to become who you need?

Who told you that love doesn't hurt?
That it's 'just down to luck' if everything works
That love doesn't need you to fight its corner
If you swim out to sea, don't blame the water

You don't get the view of the sun at sunset
If you scorch the sky each time you're upset

Who taught you not to forgive? I forget
Oh wait, I see, beneath this mess
You did love once – it left you scared
Heart all crushed inside your chest

Lost yourself and trusted less
And wow, it fucked your mental health
So you built towers and walls, a fence
And learnt this cynical defence
That you're just 'working on yourself'
And disconnected love and sex

Then each time someone you met
Knocked on the gate, you wouldn't let 'em
Step inside, put snipers on 'em,
Liked and swiped, killed, forgotten

And I know it feels naive to hope
Get bit by snake, you'll flinch at rope
But who taught you to hurt and cope
And bury all the things they broke?

Do you think, underneath it all
That all the pain is all your fault?
That just because someone abused it
That's on you? Oh, you've confused it

There's a child in you whose bruises
Needs your adult voice to soothe 'em
Love is never forced, you choose it
Love's a force of play, it's music
Who told you that love was easy?
That it's not to stand as Eve in Eden
Unguarded, naked, human, breathing
Hurting, lost and grieving, needy

It's a dangerous thing but it must be done
To stand or lie beside someone
And say 'I'm broken and so are you
Do you love me?
'Cos I'm trying to'

Why Me?

'cos you're the only one who could take it
why me?
'cos everyone else was busy
why me?
'cos you were last at the party
why me?
'cos we all break and it's your lucky day
why me?
'cos you were standing closest
why me?
'cos someone else needs to know it's survivable
why me?
it was either you or your sister
why me?
'cos you were dressed for the occasion
why me?
it wasn't you, it was your sister
why me?

why not you?
why me?
'cos you were finally ready
why me?
'cos you needed to understand
why me?
if not you, who?
why me?
'cos someone had to do it
why me?
no one else was ready
why me?
my hands were full
why me?
who else would you send?

why me?
no, who else would you send?
why me?
'cos we needed a volunteer

and the next time someone is
on the brink or on the bridge
or on the edge or in the depths

and asks 'Has anyone here made it out?
does anyone here know about pain?'

you will raise your hand in the air and say
'Why? Me.'

I don't go on walks to cheer myself up

I go on walks to feel my sadness in peace
I walk and feel as sad as I can
To acknowledge the person I already am
Who here on this planet feels kinda down

And the walk doesn't cheer me up that much
But feeling things fully
Maybe that does

In

her bedroom there's a little book
she writes the names of everyone she's ever kissed
like 'Alex, Alex, Amy, Andrew' (alphabetically like this)

and no one ever read it or knew that it exists
it wasn't all that special, it wasn't a long list

just something she did for fun
was just a thing she did

If you age seven could see you now

Would you say the truth is
Life's a sound
You forget to hear
Once you've been thrown around

Or would you pull them near
And fix their crown
And warm their hands
Speak clear and loud

And tell them 'Please never forget
You are the only you you get'

'Treat yourself like you were sent
Into the world on purpose' then
'You are not some empty thing
Some vase to hold dead flowers in

You are now and you are it'
Like 'When I grow up . . .'
You're *in* that bit

How to kill a CEO

It's easy if you try
Just keep the people nice and sick
And let their mothers die

And maybe some real handsome boy
Some leading man type guy
Will pop three rounds into his head
And no one will ask why

'Cos the answer is the question
'What's the point in trying?'
When their system needs you sick and dead
To hit their profit line

And I cannot condone murder
Before you paint me red
I just observe the consequence
Of keeping all the bread

With those who coin the suffering
Asleep on private jets
See, we grew up watching *Hunger Games*
And *The Lion King* and yet
Everyone's surprised when kids
Wanna overthrow some shit

But it's really not the murderer
Or the murder or the meme
It's the truth behind the gunshot
It's just how much we've seen

It's the feeling that they kind of
Only love you on your knees

It's your family getting sicker
Whilst they're waiting for the op
It's the feeling that the bottom's
Getting further from the top

This is how you kill a CEO
It's not by getting shot
It's by dancing whilst we bury
All the people you forgot

You wouldn't understand

Two people buy a boat
And sail it out a hundred miles

One of them is dying
And one of them's a child
And the dying man is tired
He says 'Sit with me a while'

But the child says
'I can't, I have to keep on rowing'
And the dying man says 'Oh?
And where is it you're going?'

And the child says 'Don't know
But I'm sure it will be pretty'
And the sun shone on the waves
Like lovers in the city

And the dying man says
'I'll make you a deal
I'll speak to them upstairs
To make all your dreams real

And all you have to do is sit with me
And remember how this feels'
And the child says 'Fine'
And they sit silent for some time

Then the dying man says
'Well I best be getting going'
And the child says 'Yeah
But how will I be knowing

If they grant me all I want
Will your promise stay afloat?'
And the dying man says
'How'd you think we got this boat?'

Recovery

Happiness is not a debt
that needs to be paid back
in misery or misfortune

Hunger

The last time you looked at me I nearly fell apart
Today I'm counting lucky stars because
I've already seen you eat
So I don't have to ask

We're just some faded candles and scars
But these times the mornings seem just as dark
To wake up and watch you fall apart all over again
If it would sustain you
I'd pull ribbons from my chest
And feed you broken pieces of my heart

But it's not enough
It's not even a drop
Just to be here for you
You're not sleeping
I'm just waiting scared to death
You're gonna take a breath
In case I miss it
And I'll have never witnessed the last
Time your lungs dragged a whirlwind
Girl when I was standing by your side afraid of catching faces
In the street as you walk from A to being
More than just your disorders
As you trace the floor with pencil legs and sunken chest
'Are you hungry?' someone asks as they walk past
And they have that same look on their face
And it's disgusting no one discussed this with you
Maybe the deepest pain to date

But this is not a heart to break
This is basic
This is you and I face to face with
This together
Until your paper weight drops again
And I will stand and pick you up again
And if you need to rest then listen darling you rest hard
If I stand beside your bed, am I your guardian, your guard
Is it my war to fight the devil in your mind
Or am I just forever making this about me all the time
Scratching at the outside of your skull
Like a child at a shop window,
Writing this crossing rivers, killing killers
Somehow believing I'm the star
She shines in lethal doses
No serotonin here
I'll be the atmosphere
Around you keeping warmth inside
Deflecting bad ideas
Busy tube feeding through your nose
But you can hold my arm
I'll fight even if I'm disarmed
Until there's nothing left to harm you
Counting stars for you
Pick me constellations darling

Are you listening?
Darling darling darling
It doesn't sound right when I say it
This thing doesn't sound right when I play it
Because you are not art
This cannot be romanticised
If it was this and being rich I'd still be poor

Fuck your '90s model talk
Shit ain't sexy any more
This is not some minority issue any more

So why the fuck am I still scared to ask
And after lunch we'd sit and laugh
You used to dance
You used to ask me things
You used to cook
I nearly laughed writing this

Because when food becomes the enemy
The absence of your energy
Becomes the centre of the dark
And then the hunger's undecidedly
The make-up of your mask
When people ask you say
'Oh no I've already eaten'
And on occasions unavoidable
You plunge your fingers so far down your throat
You'd think you were trying to reach your heart
Finger thumb palpitations just to kickstart arteries but never art
I'd love to see you dance again
I'd love to see you do that Rachel laugh from *Friends*
But it's all so fragile
Pencil legs and porcelain skin
You slowly blink just to invite me in

'Cos words are hard to come by when your body's bleeding inwards
And people say shit like well that girl needs a few more dinners
Fuck you

Fuck you and your ignorance
Fuck you and your sleeping waste of understanding
You've never seen feet too weak to walk
So you best be very careful where you're standing
There's no safer place to grace the land with
Than right here with my hand in yours

But I can't write your stories
I can't make your mornings
I can't take it all in
I can only be here
And it's not enough
You open your mouth to speak, half asleep
Hallucinating now
System shutting down
Without a doubt I'm certain
Today your life is ending
This is Independence Day
Another way to say within the next few hours
People will be placing flowers
At your doorstep saying 'I had no idea'

And I'll say I know
How could you
Why would you
Why should anyone ask
Such a simple question
It's the hardest thing to say
Are you okay

But then the clouds crack, it's judgment day
A flash of lightning in her eyes, a ray
Parts her lips, she says
'Yeah yeah, I'm dying. But not today
I'll tell you when I'm done, just wait
You don't start counting down 'til I say
Don't ever leave me in a room with some faith
'Cos I will change what can't be changed
Yeah yeah, I'm dying. Fucking ay,
But let me die in a beautiful place
Think of it more as waking up
Think of a future paved with love
And things to do and bite and hug'

And so today I know I'm blessed
'Cos for the first time you looked at me
With hunger in your chest

**No such thing as
the one that got away**

'cos the one
the one

the one fucking stays

They look down at us from up there

Saying 'Bless them, let them play'
Like a child with a plastic oven
Tryna bake a cake

And taking it so seriously
All screwing up our face
And crying when confronted
With a world we can't explain

And probably some time from now
Our facts will sound so quaint
And spoken of how we think of
Leeches curing plague

And hope that they forgive us
For the things we desecrate
And placing all our value
On how much cash we make

And missing all the points
Of this miracle we raid
I hope someone up there speaks for us
And all we lay to waste

Saying 'Judge them not too harshly
They're just lost in the game
And born into such broken things
Which they perpetuate'

But nothing scares me more than
The thought of some last day
When the sky cracks open
Thunderclouds of fire blaze away

A hand reaches down
Says 'Come with us, we'll take you home now safe'

And one of us goes
'Ehh, I don't know, how much does it pay?'

The plot of *Dune*

Spend a little time with the enemy
And you'll find out who's the enemy

(all the mixed-race boys) Audition

You used to be able to get water here
There was a little cupboard in the corner
And you'd shuffle past all the nervous same font faces
And me I'd try to fill up as much space as possible
Because I felt deserving of so little

I jumped the train to get here
But if I get this little crisp advert
I'll be the richest person I know
I'll make what our dads made in a year in two days
(Didn't get it) jumped the train home
Five-hour round trip, got caught, fined £200
Used to see Jason and Jordan and Sam
At every audition, all the mixed-race boys

That was half a decade and a million years ago
Don't see anyone anywhere now
Statistically speaking they can't avoid me !
I'm always somewhere on someone's screen

Back when that Ariel girl lived on billboards
And that freckled girl had Michael Caine's agent
She was in that car commercial for £15K (Europe / inc. cinemas)
This was the pre-autoimmune disease era
There really hasn't been one second of my life
That's been a problem outside of my mind

I wanted some water
But that little cupboard doesn't exist now
So I just sat and waited patiently
To embarrass myself for three minutes

And I should thank that boy
Just nineteen years of age
For fighting half to death
For me to live today

The world got smaller

just as you left
and me, I got taller

so now,
if there's someone I miss
I just call them

miracles

walking around the house in a bath towel
with wet hair & saying
'i will actually fucking finally fucking switch'

best life of my life
the way the last of the sun hits the piano upstairs,
she's a bird, it's a treehouse

balcony video, oh Juliet, bet
a stranger at the airport congratulated us
she wished us a beautiful marriage
'why does the shawl make it feel more romantic'

Bella Hadid liked the video, classic
I wanna Tilly Losch her footsteps on the carpet

and all of my writing
or thinking or fighting
was always really
just to find her

Act III

I want you to make it, I want you there to see it
In your best Sunday best when the sun explodes
And all the sky a firework, I want to see you seeing it
Baby blue translucent you gripping onto your sweetheart
Darling honey thank you – you – angel, all the same word
There at the finale

I want the choir to know the song we need
The cut marks on your arms are glitter gold
A pathway through a video game forest
I want to say I'm sorry, I'm sorry for not seeing sooner
I'm sorry I was scared and newer than I thought

I'm sorry I was quiet in rooms that carry sound
I'm sorry I'm a liar in ways I'll never understand
I'm sorry we are all the same – I grew up in your town

I want you to make it
I love that feeling man
A hundred million faces
The end, the end, the now

I found God at the funeral

He was up by the snacks
Not at the church – the bit after that
When you go to a function room in the rain
Eat little cakes in a suit, feel strange
I thought 'Why is He here when He's to blame?
Talking so loud all over our pain
Like a serial killer suspect in a case
Pulling up eating pastries at the wake'

So I said 'I'm not having it, not today'
Slammed the plate from his hands
Said 'You should be ashamed
How dare you even show your face
You wander around like a King on parade
And want us to thank you for all of our pain
Well never again, nuh-uh, no way
I think you should leave, fuck off, go away'

And he looked at me straight
I was shaking with rage
And he said something then that I can't explain
He said 'Blessed are we, who know our name'

And I said 'Fuck that, no, no more games
I won't be soothed or softened or changed
Or manipulated by poetic refrains
Just leave us alone, just leave this place
How dare you leave children buried in graves
How dare you leave widows, grow hearts to break
How dare you, God damn you
And damn you again'

And my chest was trembling catching its air
God said 'Are you done?'
I said 'I think so, yeah'

And he pulled out two of those stackable chairs
He patted the first, said 'Come rest, there'
He cracked me a can, which I thought was weird
'Ain't it usually wine?'
He said 'I've only got beers'

He said 'Man, I'm sorry
I know it's confusing
To give you a life that you're always losing
But you're part of a network – your role is human

You're here to make all the wonder make sense
You're not the life – you're the *living* itself
Who told you that death was an end?
With a million years, you won't comprehend

The complexity, majesty, awe of it all
You call it Autumn, others say Fall
You call it a life, some call it a wall
It's beautiful really, I guess it's my fault

I taught you to wonder and break all the rules
But you have to admit, it is pretty cool
To live and then disappear into a storm
What value is life that can't be mourned

And this thing you all do where you see me and hide
It's peek-a-boo – cute, but I'm here the whole time
As if all of those days you spent broken at home
Were spent by yourself – you were never alone'

Then I looked at the cups and the paper plates
The tray of red velvet that someone had baked
I looked at the shoes of the men, all laced
And the women with dresses and faces all made

The kids in a makeshift plastic playroom
Not knowing, thinking 'Which one is the main groom?'
I looked at the faces of people I loved
Who dressed and drove, brought food, turned up

I looked at the wonder of all of this fuss
I looked back at God, I said 'Fair enough
But when it's my time, please God, be soft
I cannot bear them hurting this much'

He smiled a moment then said 'Best be off'
I said 'Where are you going?'
He said 'It's our stop.'

And it felt like a dance or a firework show
It felt like – well, one day you'll know
It felt like a man with a plate at a funeral
Like thank you for coming
I hope it was beautiful

Acknowledgements

This book would not exist without the love, faith and grace of so many people. With infinite gratitude and appreciation, thank you all forever.

Thank you to my wonderful agent Alice Welby at Kruger Cowne for catching the vision from the very beginning. A constant reminder that trust, good instincts and good people will always lead to beautiful things. For your endless support and for guiding this project with such elegance and care.

To my amazing editor, Amanda Waters at Ebury. Thank you for your infinite positivity, kindness and razor-sharp insight throughout this dream of a process. For sensing the reason for this book and the hours and months spent nurturing and discovering its heart. *For choosing to love despite it all.* Thank you, always.

Special thanks to Jessica Anderson for your patience and attention to every line and detail.

Thank you to Loulou Clark for all of your insight and direction in creating the visual world of this book.

Thank you also to Jessica Patel for your help.

Thank you also to Zoë Jellicoe and Kay Delves for, quite literally, crossing the t's and dotting the i's.

Thank you to Chad Moore. For the endless inspiration of your work and a manic few days in NYC shooting the cover of this book. (Climbing rooftops with Chad Moore – *oh, dreams do come true.*)

Thank you also to Delaney Anderson for all of your help in NYC.

Thank you to Jamie Keenan for sharing your vision, precision and talent in creating the front cover of this book.

Thank you to the publicity team at Ebury, Penguin Random House, especially Francesca Thomson and Margarida Mendes Ribeiro, for your hard work and care throughout the launch. I'm endlessly grateful for your enthusiasm and effort in this book finding its people.

To every single person who has helped to build this strange and beautiful revolution of 21st-century poetry over the last few years. For reading, sharing, watching, buying or tattooing any of my work, you have my unending gratitude for life. It means more than I can comprehend. Thank you.

To Shean Williams for a million hours of soul searching and a million more of soul saving. Thank you, brother. Clean game, always.

To Dean Graham for (very genuinely) keeping me from losing my mind in this mad city. A billion years, on some Zargon IIV shit.

To Leo Flanagan, for walking every street of London until the chaos subsides and the girls are out shopping. For dreaming and keeping the dreams alive. STARmeter forever.

To my dad, for your endless support and faith. For placing films and music and books in the hands and heart of a child so beautifully, it became my entire world. For constantly sharing the inspiration of art and tirelessly encouraging my creativity. I owe you more than you will accept and I love you.

To my mum, for being the living manifestation of love. Any compassion and empathy I have in this world are yours. Thank you for sharing the delusion of my ambitions until they become reality. Thank you for protecting my heart in the world. It's an honour to be your son. I love you.

To my brother, for everything. For always, always being there. Before I was trying to be me, I was mainly just trying to be you. Got used to it in the end, though, Hartford shop and Nightfire ones and that.

To my sister, an angel and somehow my boss and manager since she was six ... Forever proud and inspired by you. The best, the best.

And finally, to my love, Lily. Your name is the word I've been looking for forever. Thank you for bringing all of the colour, wonder and beauty into my life. I did not know peace before you. Some little dragon, some big dream, I swear to God I will switch right now. I love you forever.

About the author

Lucas Jones is a London-based actor and poet whose work captures the cultural moment with precision and relevance. Writing in real time through social media, Lucas explores themes of masculinity, love, grief and connection, offering a perspective that feels both thoughtful and immediate. In addition to his poetry, Lucas has earned recognition as an actor across many film and TV projects and for his work as a director and screenplay writer.